TERRA THE TRICERATOPS' LUNCH ADVENTURE

CRUNCH!

MUNCH!

CHOMP!

Written & Designed
by
Latoya Belfon-John,
Khai-El John
Kaleel John

ISBN: 978-1-990420-21-4

LAB WORKS
PUBLISHING

It was lunchtime, and Terra the Triceratops took a quick walk to find some yummy plants to eat. As she wandered, she reached a shimmering lagoon, where the water sparkled under the warm sun.

In the shallow water, she spotted a parrotfish named Ella swimming nearby.

Hi Ella! Do you know where I can find some yummy plants to eat?

Terra asked.

Did you know? 🦕 Triceratops had 800 teeth that never stopped growing!

Ella flicked her fins.

Hmm... I don't know where to find plants, but I do know of a beautiful coral reef with yummy plankton!

Terra tilted her head.

Plankton? Is that tasty?

My whale friend says it's delicious!

Terra shook her head.

Oh no! I can't swim.

Ella sighed.

With a flick of her tail, she swam away.

Cool Fact! 🐠 Parrotfish sleep in a bubble of slime at night to hide from predators!

Disappointed but determined, Terra continued her search. Soon, she saw a long neck stretching high into the trees.

Heyyyyyy! Heeyyy up there?

she called.

Brady the Brachiosaurus, bent his long neck down.

Heyyyyyy down there!

I'm looking for some yummy plants to eat! Do you know where I can find some?

"Of course! I have a delicious buffet up here. These leaves are the best! Why don't you join me?

Terra sighed.

Oh no! I'm too short to reach.

Sorry Terra! Hope you find some yummy plants!

If only I were taller!

She stared longingly at the leafy branches, their bright green leaves rustling above her. she thought.

Awesome Fact! 🦕 Brachiosaurus was as tall as a four-story building and had front legs longer than its back legs—just like a giraffe!

After leaving the Brachiosaurus, Terra's tummy rumbled louder than a volcano.

RUMBLE!

She sighed. Would she ever find something to eat?

Did you know? 🦖 Triceratops loved to eat tough plants like ferns, cycads, and ginkgo leaves like in the picture above!

oh no!

Can't swim!

oh no!

Too ⌐ short

What will Terra do?
Just then, she heard a loud

CRUNCH!!

It sounded like big teeth chomping on yummy leaves! Terra rushed off, hoping to find someone who could help.

WHOOSH!

But instead, she saw a Pterosaur preparing for takeoff! His wings flapped so hard, they made a whooshing sound.

"Hey there! Do you know where I can find some yummy plants?"

she shouted.

But the Pterosaur, Peter, couldn't hear her over the wind from his wings.

Just as he was about to take off, Terra jumped in front of him!

AHHHH!

Peter wobbled and tumbled to the ground. Terra gasped.

Oh no! I'm so sorry for startling you.

Phew! That was close. Hi, I'm Peter the Pterosaur. What can I help you with?

Peter shook himself off.

I'm Terra the Triceratops! I'm looking for some yummy plants to eat, but I can't find any.

Parrotfish tried to help, but I couldn't swim. The Brachiosaurus tried to help, but I was too short to reach. Can you help me?

Peter tapped his beak.

Hmmm... I know! I'll fly up high and scope out some plants for you. Wait here!

With a flap of his wings, Peter soared into the sky. He circled and scanned the land below.

A few moments later, he zoomed back down.

I found some! And something even better! Follow me!

Terra's tummy gave a little roar. She galloped after Peter as fast as she could.

Awesome Fact! Pterosaurs were the first reptiles to ever fly! Some had wingspans as wide as a school bus, while others were as small as a pigeon.

Soon, she was surrounded by beautiful, yummy plants! Just as she was about to take a big bite, she heard a familiar voice.

"Terra?"

She turned around. It was her dad!

"Terra! There you are! Come join us—we found the yummiest plants just for you!"

Terra beamed. After her long adventure, this was the yummiest lunch ever! Her family was so happy to see her, and they dived into lunch...

CRUNCH!

MUNCH!

CHOMP!

HYPOTHETICAL FACTS ABOUT THE TRICERATOPS' FRILL

1. **Defense:** It may have helped protect its neck from predators like T. rex.

2. **Communication:** Some scientists believe it may have changed colours to signal danger, attract mates, or show dominance.

3. **Temperature Control:** The frill could have helped regulate body heat, like how modern elephants use their ears.

FRILL

Feed The Dino!

"FEED THE DINOSAURS! WHO EATS WHAT?"

Draw a line to connect each dinosaur to the meal they would eat!

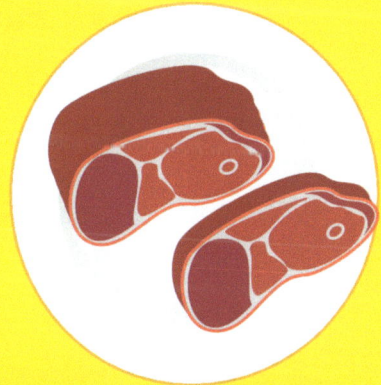

All of Our Books

COLOR ME COCO COLORING BOOK

Available at Walmart.com

Color Me Coco

Mom, Can you Tell me a Story? The Lost Little Lion Cub

MY DAD THE SUPERHERO

A Tale of Two Creations! COCO & YURIKO

GO TO SLEEP LITTLE ONE

Available at **BARNES & NOBLE**

THE REAL EASTER STORY COLOURING BOOK!

Best Seller amazon.ca

GRANDMA'S HAND

Best Seller amazon.ca

IZZY'S NEW LIFE The Way I Talk by Latoya Belfon

MOMMY LOVES BABY

Cadence Learns Self-Love

I JUST LOVE CHRISTMAS

Where Flies The Bird?

THE LOST LITTLE LION CUB'S BIG ADVENTURE! by Latoya Belfon

Available at **amazon**

Visit Our Youtube Channel

Watch & Enjoy More Stories on Story Land Playground!

Love The Lion Cub's Big Adventure? The fun doesn't stop here! Join us on our YouTube channel, Story Land Playground, where stories come to life with exciting read-alouds, engaging animations, and fun-filled learning adventures!

🔹 **What You'll Find on Story Land Playground:**

✅ Read-Along Story Videos – Enjoy beautifully narrated read-alouds of your favorite books!

✅ Interactive Learning – Fun quizzes, educational videos, and exciting activities for kids!

✅ Music & Movement – Sing, dance, and learn with catchy songs and kid-friendly content!

✅ Confidence & Creativity Boosters – Fun challenges, storytelling tips, and writing activities to inspire young minds!

Perfect for Kids Ages 3-10, Parents, Teachers & Librarians!

📣 Visit us on YouTube today!

🎬 Watch the read-aloud version of this book and discover more amazing content!

SCAN ME

SUBSCRIBE

SHARE

LIKE

www.ingramcontent.com/pod-product-compliance
Lightning Source LLC
Chambersburg PA
CBHW042110040426
42448CB00002B/209